WE COME FROM

China

JULIA WATERLOW

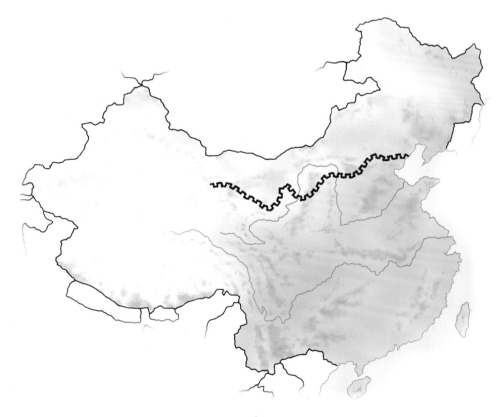

HODDER
Wayland

an imprint of Hodder Children's Books

WE COME FROM

Brazil • China • France
Germany • India • Jamaica • Japan
Kenya • Nigeria • South Africa

Most of the people you are about to meet live in a village in China called Dragon's Village. Like any country, China has many different types of lifestyles. People live in towns and cities as well as in villages.

Cover: Feifei and two of her friends stand in front of the hills around Dragon's Village.

Title page (from top to bottom): A farmer returns from the market; high-rise buildings fill the skyline in Shanghai; a Chinese Opera character entertains an audience in Shanghai; shoppers in a busy market hunt for bargains; and Tiananmen Gate in Beijing.

Contents page: A woman carries some goods to sell at the local market.

Index: Feifei waves goodbye.

All Wayland books encourage children to read and help them improve their literacy.

✓ The contents page, page numbers, headings and index help locate specific pieces of information.

✓ The glossary reinforces alphabetic knowledge and extends vocabulary.

✓ The further information section suggests other books dealing with the same subject.

Series editor: Katie Orchard
Designer: Jean Wheeler
Production controller: Tracy Fewtrell

Picture Acknowledgements: All the photographs in this book were taken by Gordon Clements except for Wayland Picture Library (Richard Sharpley) page 14 (top). Artwork was produced by Peter Bull (page 5) and Kate Davenport (page 28).

First published in Great Britain in 1999 by Wayland Publishers Limited
This paperback edition published in 2002 by Hodder Wayland, an imprint of Hodder Children's Books
© Hodder Wayland 1999

Hodder Children's Books
A division of Hodder Headline Limited
338 Euston Road, London NW1 3BH

British Library Cataloguing in Publication Data
Waterlow, Julia
  We come from China
  1. China – Geography – Juvenile literature
  2. China – Social conditions – 1976– – Juvenile literature
  I. Title II. China
  951' .059
  ISBN 0 7502 4386 4

Printed and bound in Hong Kong

Contents

Introduction   4

The Land and Weather   6

At Home   10

Food and Cooking   14

Working Hard   18

School   20

Spare Time   24

Looking Ahead   26

Chinese Writing   28

China Fact File   29

Topic Web   30

Extension Activities   30

Glossary   31

Further Information   31

Index   32

Introduction

'I live with my parents, my sister Fong, and my uncle's family.' Feifei.

▲ *From left to right:*
Xui (Feifei's uncle)
Fong (Feifei's sister)
Feifei
Xue (Feifei's cousin)
Sau Ling (Feifei's auntie)

Feifei is nine years old. She lives in a village in southern China called Dragon's Village. You can see where it is on the map on page five. Feifei's family are farmers. They grow vegetables, fruit and rice.

▶ *China's place in the world.*

▼ *China is a very big country. More people live there than in any other country in the world.*

CHINA

Capital city:	Beijing
Land area:	9,597,000 square kilometres
Population:	1,300,000,000 people
Main language:	Mandarin Chinese
Main religion:	Buddhism, although most people are not very religious

The Land and Weather

Most people live in the eastern half of China, nearest to the sea. The land is fairly flat here and it is easier to grow food.

There are high mountains and deserts in the rest of China. Few people live there. It is too high and cold in the mountains to grow much, and in the deserts it is too dry.

▲ A dam on the Yangzi River. Boats can sail far inland along the river.

► The Chinese cut terraces into hillsides so that they can grow rice, even in the hills.

◄ China has some of the highest mountains in the world.

Winter in the north is freezing cold. Often there is snow and ice. But summers can be hot, dry and dusty. In southern China the weather is warm all year round.

▲ *A boy wraps up in a coat and hat to keep out the cold in north China.*

▶ *It often rains in the south of China.*

The farmers in Feifei's village grow rice. It needs warm weather and plenty of rain to grow. There are many rivers near Dragon's Village. There are hills all around and the villagers think one of these looks like a dragon. That's how the village got its name.

'I helped to harvest this big basket of rice.' Feifei.

At Home

Towns and cities in China are very crowded. Most people live in blocks of flats. Families usually have two or three small rooms. Many city people have televisions and some have washing machines.

▼ *This boy lives in a flat. His family has a colour television and modern furniture.*

▲ *Flats often have balconies. Lots of people hang out their washing on their balconies.*

In the countryside most people live in houses. Few houses have bathrooms or inside toilets. Many villagers collect water every day from wells or taps in their village.

▼ *Children play outside a country house.*

◀ *People wash clothes and vegetables in the village stream.*

Feifei's house has a high brick wall around it. Inside there are two buildings. One is for her family and the other is for her uncle's family. Feifei shares a bedroom with her older sister, Fong. Her family has one other bedroom, and a living room where everyone eats and talks together.

▼ *Feifei's family has a pet owl. It catches mice.*

'I sometimes help my parents by collecting firewood for cooking.' Feifei.

13

Food and Cooking

People in southern China usually eat rice with their meals. In the north, most people have noodles. The Chinese eat vegetables, meat, fish or eggs with their rice or noodles.

▲ *Noodles are made from flour. These noodles are drying in the hot sunshine.*

◀ *In the cities there are hundreds of small snack stalls, such as this one.*

▶ *Duck is a favourite Chinese dish. There are lots of duck farms around village areas.*

15

Chinese food is chopped into small pieces so that it cooks quickly. Lots of different dishes are put in the middle of the table so that everyone can help themselves.

◀ *Feifei's uncle often does the cooking for his family, using a wok.*

'I use chopsticks to pick up my food.' Feifei.

Farmers come to the market to sell fresh vegetables.

Feifei's family doesn't have a fridge so they usually eat fresh or dried food. They grow a lot of it themselves. Feifei's mum goes shopping at the village market once a week to buy the extra things they need.

Working Hard

In Dragon's Village many people are farmers like Feifei's family. They grow crops and keep some animals. Farmers hoe the ground by hand and use animals to plough the land.

'It's hard work growing rice but it's a good harvest this year so we're happy.' Feifei's mum.

▲ *Builders work on a house near Dragon's Village.*

In the cities, people hurry to work in shops, offices and factories. Many people are leaving the countryside to live and work in the cities, where they can earn more money.

▶ *In cities few people have cars. Many ride to work on bicycles instead.*

School

Chinese children go to school from the age of six or seven. Some village schools have only stools, a few desks and one or two books. City schools can be quite different, with very modern equipment.

▼ *A modern city school with computers.*

▲ *These students are having extra lessons at the weekend.*

Chinese and maths are the main subjects. Many Chinese children are now learning English. They also play sports, such as basketball. There are two school holidays each year – one in summer and one in winter.

▼ *Most schools have a playground with a basketball net.*

'I ride to school on my bicycle every morning.' Feifei.

Feifei's first lesson starts at eight o'clock in the morning and she has two hours off for lunch. School finishes at four o'clock and then she goes home to do her homework.

▼ *In fine weather children often do their homework outside.*

Feifei gets up at half-past five in the morning to feed the chickens. After school she looks after the pigs. Some village schools close during harvest time so that the children can help their parents to get the crops in.

▲ *After school, this boy looks after his family's buffalo.*

Spare Time

Many Chinese people love to spend their free time watching television.

In the cities, the parks are often crowded with families spending time together. Sometimes there is music, dancing or an acrobatic show to watch.

▲ *A group of friends play the Chinese game Mahjong.*

'I spend most of my spare time playing in the fields outside.' Feifei.

▶ *This boy is spinning a home-made wooden top.*

Looking Ahead

China has changed a lot in the last few years. Life for ordinary Chinese people is getting better all the time. People in the cities are becoming more modern, as they find out about life in other countries.

▲ Mobile phones are becoming popular in China's cities.

▼ *Modern skyscrapers tower above the city of Shanghai.*

'I want to be a singer when I get older. I practise by singing to Xue.' Feifei.

27

Chinese Writing

Chinese children learn characters instead of an alphabet. Each character stands for a word.

• This character is the word for person: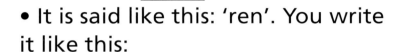

• It is said like this: 'ren'. You write it like this:

First line   Second line

• This is the character for big:

• It is said like this: 'da'. To write it you just add a third line to the character for person.

•Put both characters together to get the word for grown-up: 'da ren'. Try writing them yourself.

▲ *Feifei writes her own name in Chinese.*

China Fact File

Money Facts China's money is the Yuan. £1 is worth about 10 Yuan.

Mountain Facts The highest mountain in China is Mount Everest in the Himalayas (8,848 metres high).

River Facts China's longest river is the Yangzi River (6,300 kilometres long).

▲ The Yellow River is another long river. It is 5,464 kilometres long.

◀ **Flag** The Chinese flag is red with five yellow stars. One star is for the Communist Party and the others represent soldiers, peasants, workers and students.

▼ **Pandas** Giant pandas are found only in China. There are not many left and they are protected.

Famous People Mao Zedong ▶ (1893–1976) was a famous Chinese leader who led the Communist Party. Confucius was a famous wise man born in about 551 BC.

Inventions The Chinese invented many things, including paper, gunpowder and silk.

Holidays The most important holiday is Chinese New Year which usually takes place in early February. There are special lion and dragon dances, street processions and fireworks.

▲ **Great Wall** Parts of the Great Wall of China are over 2,000 years old. It is the only building in the world that can be seen from space.

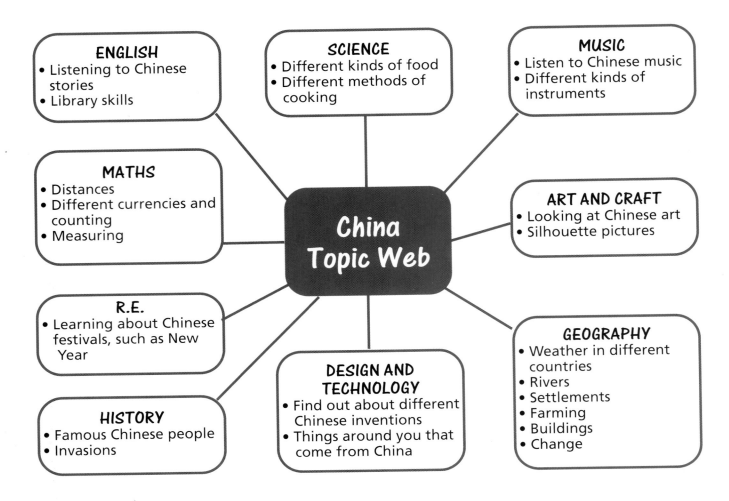

ENGLISH
- Listening to Chinese stories
- Library skills

SCIENCE
- Different kinds of food
- Different methods of cooking

MUSIC
- Listen to Chinese music
- Different kinds of instruments

MATHS
- Distances
- Different currencies and counting
- Measuring

China Topic Web

ART AND CRAFT
- Looking at Chinese art
- Silhouette pictures

R.E.
- Learning about Chinese festivals, such as New Year

GEOGRAPHY
- Weather in different countries
- Rivers
- Settlements
- Farming
- Buildings
- Change

HISTORY
- Famous Chinese people
- Invasions

DESIGN AND TECHNOLOGY
- Find out about different Chinese inventions
- Things around you that come from China

Extension Activities

GEOGRAPHY
- Do we eat any foods that come from China? Investigate packets and labels.
- Talk about why most people in cities live in flats, while those in rural areas tend to live in houses.

DESIGN AND TECHNOLOGY
- Discuss some Chinese inventions.

ENGLISH
- Write a postcard to a friend telling them about what it's like in Dragon's Village.
- Read the story of the *Monkey King*.

SCIENCE
- Make a Chinese recipe, such as a noodle dish.

MATHS
- Try to work out how much certain items cost in Chinese Yuan.

ART AND CRAFT
- Look at Chinese art, such as silhouette pictures.
- Try to draw the characters on page 28.

Glossary

Acrobats Entertainers with amazing gymnastic skills.

Buffalo The kind of buffalo you see in China is a water buffalo. It is a cow with big horns.

Chopsticks A pair of thin sticks that Chinese people use to pick up their food.

Communist People who belong to the Communist political party. They believe that money and work should be shared out equally.

Dam A barrier built to hold back water and stop flooding.

Deserts Places where few plants grow because it is very dry.

Hoe To weed the ground using a tool with a long handle.

Terraces Flat areas of land cut into a hillside. It is easier to grow things if the land is flat.

Wells Deep holes in the ground that you can get water out of.

Further Information

Information Books
C is for China by Sungwan So (Frances Lincoln, 1997)
Country Fact Files: China by Catherine Charley (MacDonald Young Books, 1994)
Country Insights: China by Julia Waterlow (Wayland, 1996)
A Family from China by Julia Waterlow (Wayland, 1998)
Look into the Past: the Ancient Chinese by Julia Waterlow (Wayland, 1994)
Our Country: China by Julia Waterlow (Wayland, 1991)

Fiction
Chinese Myths and Legends retold by Philip Ardagh (Belitha Press, 1996)
The Emperor and the Nightingale by Meilo So (Frances Lincoln, 1997)

Useful Addresses
Cultural Section, Chinese Embassy, 11 West Heath Road, London NW3.

The Great Britain-China Centre, 15 Belgrave Square, London SW1X 8PS.

Index

All the numbers in **bold** refer to photographs.

animals 18
  buffalo **23**
  chickens 23
  ducks 14, **15**
  pigs 23
  pandas 29, **29**

bicycles **19**, **22**
Beijing 5

chopsticks 16, **16**
cities 10, 14, 19, **19**, 20, 24, 26, **26**
crops 18, 23

Dragon's Village 4, 9

deserts 6

flag 29
flats 10, **10**
food 14–17
  noodles 14, **14**
  rice 4, 6, 9, **9**, 14, **18**
  vegetables 4, **12**, 14, **17**

Great Wall **5**, 29, **29**

harvest 18, **18**, 23
holidays 21, 29
houses 11, **11**, 12, **19**

markets 17, **17**

money 29
mountains 6, **6**, 29

school 20, 21 **20**, **21**, 22, 23
Shanghai **26**

television 10, **10**, 24
terraces **6**

villages 9, 11, 20

weather 6, 8, 9, 22
writing 28, **28**

Yangzi River 6, 29
Yellow River **29**